I0814289

CHEERLEADING

SPIRIT-RAISING CHEERS AND CHANTS

By India James

SportsZone
An Imprint of Abdo Publishing
abdobooks.com

abdobooks.com

Printed in the United States of America, North Mankato, Minnesota
052024
092024

Cover Photo: John Byrum/Icon Sportswire/AP Images
Interior Photos: Brian Bahr/Getty Images Sport/Getty Images, 4–5; Phelan M. Ebenhack/AP Images, 6; Brett Carlsen/Getty Images Sport/Getty Images, 8–9; Matthew Holst/Getty Images Sport/Getty Images, 10; Shutterstock Images, 12, 21; Rebecca Blackwell/AP Images, 15; Lee Coleman/Icon Sportswire/AP Images, 16–17; Frank Jansky/Icon Sportswire/AP Images, 18; Ian Johnson/Icon Sportswire/Getty Images, 19; Paul Kitagaki Jr./ZUMA Press Wire/Newscom, 23; Isaiah Vazquez/Getty Images Sport/Getty Images, 24–25; Keith Birmingham/MediaNews Group/Pasadena Star-News/Getty Images, 26; Michael Allio/Icon Sportswire/AP Images, 28

Editor: Christa Kelly
Series Designer: Kate Liestman

Library of Congress Control Number: 2023949604

Library of Congress Cataloging-in-Publication Data

Names: James, India, author.
Title: Spirit-raising cheers and chants / by India James
Description: Minneapolis, Minnesota: Abdo Publishing, 2025 | Series: Cheerleading | Includes online resources and index.
Identifiers: ISBN 9781098293536 (lib. bdg.) | ISBN 9798384912804 (ebook)
Subjects: LCSH: Cheerleading--Juvenile literature. | Cheers--Juvenile literature. | Yells--Juvenile literature. | Sports--Juvenile literature.
Classification: DDC 791.6--dc23

TABLE OF CONTENTS

CHAPTER 1

CHEERS AND CHANTS

Cheerleaders are known for their beautiful routines and inspiring cheers. Whether cheerleaders are performing an elaborate dance or flipping high in the air, they're impossible to ignore. It takes determination, skill, and courage to be a cheerleader. It also takes a lot of practice. Most cheerleading teams practice at least four times each week, often for two to three hours. Cheerleaders also often exercise on their own to stay fit.

A cheer team might have as many as 50 chants and cheers prepared for each game.

OSU

In some competitions, cheerleaders earn points for clear, loud cheers.

There are several different types of cheerleaders. Some cheerleaders perform for a school. They entertain audiences during games and cheer on their teams to victory. Other cheerleaders compete at cheer competitions. Still others cheer professionally at big sports games.

Cheers and chants are important parts of cheerleading. For competition cheerleaders, performing cheers and chants is a way to impress judges. For school cheerleaders and professional cheerleaders, shouting encouragement to a team and leading the crowd are among their biggest responsibilities during games. Cheers and chants can entertain a crowd and promote team spirit.

It takes a lot of hard work to learn the many cheers and chants cheerleaders have to know. It can be even harder to come up with original cheers. Perfecting cheers and chants is one of the many steps toward becoming a cheerleader.

CHAPTER 2

THE BASICS OF CHEERING AND CHANTING

Cheerleaders perform rousing chants and motivating cheers. They use cheers and chants to energize audiences and players. Though cheers and chants may sound similar, they're each used in different situations.

Chants are shorter than cheers, and they're usually repeated. Cheerleaders use chants to create short bursts of excitement. They often repeat chants at least three or four times in a row.

Cheerleaders must be physically fit in order to perform complicated skills and shout at the same time.

GO
SYRACUSE

Cheerleaders often perform cheers before a game begins to keep the crowd entertained.

Arm motions and leg motions are often used to help emphasize a team's chants.

Cheers are longer than chants. They might have several lines that rhyme. They often include the team's name. Each cheer is usually performed once. Cheerleaders often pair cheers with stunts and jumps. Because cheers are longer, cheerleaders use cheers when they have more time. Timeouts and halftimes are great opportunities for cheers.

HOW TO CHEER AND CHANT

Before cheerleaders can perform cheers and chants, they must learn the words and rhythm. Cheerleaders can bring notebooks to practice to write down any new cheers or chants. A coach might also videotape new cheers and chants. Cheerleaders can then practice them at home. Once the team has the cheers and chants memorized, they can practice

!

THE NATIONAL CHEERLEADING ASSOCIATION

Lawrence Herkimer was a cheerleader. He stuttered as a child but found that he could speak without a stutter when he was shouting cheers. In 1948, Herkimer founded the National Cheerleading Association. The organization hosts cheerleading camps, workshops, and competitions.

performing the shouts with movements. They can practice these at home in front of a mirror.

When rehearsing, cheerleaders need to practice being loud. Games are filled with excitement and noise, which can make it hard for the crowd to hear what the cheerleaders are saying. They must shout loudly and confidently to get the crowd's attention.

Coaches evaluate each applicant's projection when choosing a team.

However, cheerleaders should avoid screaming. Screaming can injure the vocal cords, the muscles in a person's throat that create sound. Instead, cheerleaders should use projection. Projection is a way of speaking that makes a person's voice louder and easier to hear from far away. To project, cheerleaders should speak from their diaphragms. The diaphragm is a muscle that controls how air moves through the lungs. When people project, they use their diaphragms to push sound out of their bodies.

Cheerleaders can practice projection through exercises. One common exercise teaches the athletes to push out air as they shout. First, cheerleaders take a big breath. They focus on expanding their lungs. Then they push all of their air out by shouting "Ha!" Practicing projection makes it easier to shout correctly during games and competitions.

PERFORMING WHILE CHEERING AND CHANTING

Choreography is an important part of cheering and chanting. Movements help grab attention and energize crowds. They also help keep the whole team synchronized.

Clapping is one way to keep a team synchronized. When cheerleaders are clapping, their hands should be in the blade position. To make the blade position, cheerleaders flatten their hands. They then extend their fingers, keeping them in line and tight against each other.

When clapping, cheerleaders keep their elbows close to their bodies. When their fingers and palms meet for a clap, the cheerleaders' hands should be just under their chins. With the right words, a good shout, and a coordinated team, cheerleaders can get a whole stadium fired up.

KNOWING WHEN TO CHEER AND CHANT

Cheering and chanting can be fun and exciting, but it's important for cheerleaders to know when to cheer and when to stay silent. Cheerleaders can cheer and chant whenever the game is in progress. Cheering can help an audience celebrate when a team is winning or raise everyone's spirits when a team is behind. Timeouts and halftimes are also good times to cheer and chant.

There are also times when it's not a good idea to cheer. It's never appropriate to cheer when a player is injured. Instead, cheerleaders should wait

Performing routines to music is one way to keep a team synchronized.

quietly while the player is helped and then applaud the player, no matter which side the player is on. Cheerleaders should also be respectful of the game. If a big play is happening and the players need to concentrate, cheerleaders should refrain from cheering. Cheerleaders should always be paying attention to the game to make sure they don't cheer at the wrong times.

CHAPTER 3

POPULAR CHEERS AND CHANTS

There are many different cheers and chants. Some are short, and some are long. But all cheers and chants are designed to engage a crowd and rally support for a team.

POPULAR CHANTS

Chants are short. Sometimes they're only a single word. Something as simple as the word "Go!" can be used for almost any sport. Most chants are repeated three or

Repeating chants can encourage spectators to join in.

VIRGINIA

There are hundreds of cheers and chants online that cheerleaders can use.

four times, but cheerleaders can repeat short chants as many times as it takes to get a crowd excited.

Sometimes cheerleaders spell out words to make chants a little longer. For example, instead of chanting "Go!," a cheerleader may chant "G-O, go!" Other chants are longer. One popular longer chant is "Stand up and yell! Let's go, team!" This chant is longer than a single word, but it's still short enough to be repeated many times. It's popular because it can work for any sport.

Many chants don't include team names. This means they can be used for any school or team.

This is convenient for learning new chants from other cheerleaders. It can be fun to exchange chants with other cheerleading teams.

POPULAR CHEERS

Unlike chants, many cheers are customized for a particular team. Because cheers are longer than

During cheers, cheerleaders should make eye contact with the crowd.

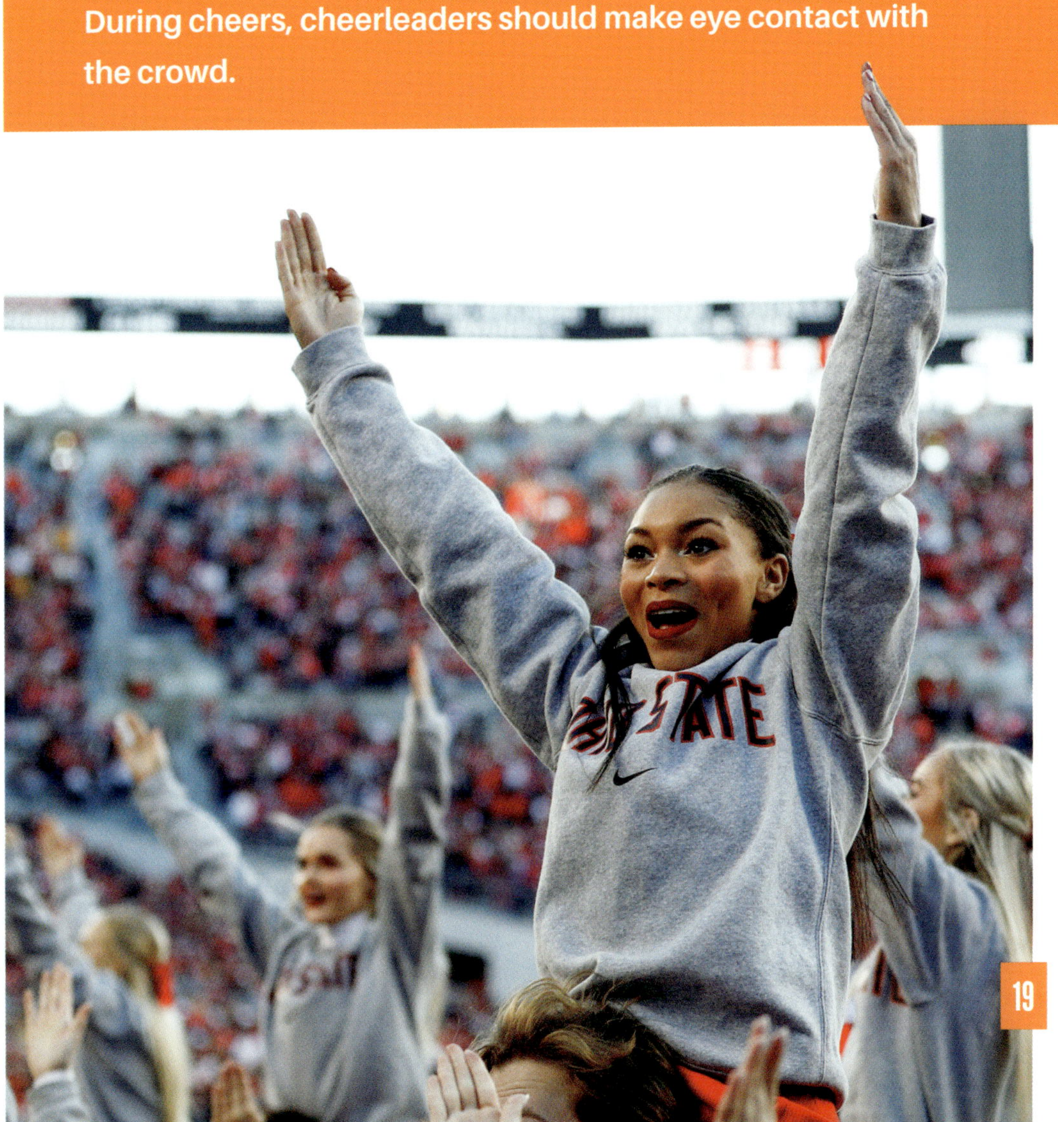

chants, they often include a team's name or a reference to a team's colors. Other cheers are specific to the sport being played. This is a great way for cheerleaders to let their team know they're being supported.

This cheer is for a team called the Kellam Knights. Because the team's name is mentioned, this is clearly a cheer meant for one specific team:

> "Go, Kellam Knights, win!
> Kellam fans, we got the beat!
> Clap your hands
> and stomp your feet!
> Go, Kellam!
> Go, Kellam!
> Kellam fans, let's hear it again,
> Clap your hands when Knights win!
> Knights win!
> Knights win!
> Go, Kellam Knights, win!"

Some cheers are designed to encourage crowd participation. This can be a great way to energize the audience. In the next example, the cheerleaders tell the crowd what to say. This is called a

In addition to leading an audience in cheers, cheerleaders can encourage an audience to clap and stomp.

call-and-response. The words in italics are said by the audience:

> "When I say go, you say fight!
> Go! *Fight!* Go! *Fight!*
> When I say win, you say tonight!
> Win! *Tonight!* Win! *Tonight!*
> When I say boogie, you say down!

Boogie! *Down!* Boogie! *Down!*
Go! Fight! Win! Tonight!
Boogie on down.
All right! All right! Go, team!"

Many schools, universities, and professional sports teams have cheers that they're known for. The first cheerleading cheers were written in the 1800s. Princeton University cheerleaders were among the first teams to make a popular cheer. They wrote cheers that sounded like the trains that brought people to and from games. Cheerleaders for Princeton University still use these cheers to motivate their teams today. This is one of their cheers. It's called "The Locomotive":

"Rah, rah, rah!
Tiger, tiger, tiger!
Sis, sis, sis!
Boom, boom, boom, ah!
Princeton! Princeton! Princeton!"

Whether new or old, cheers and chants are great ways to energize crowds and motivate teams.

Princeton University cheers often include mentions of tigers, the school's mascot.

CHAPTER 4

HOW TO MAKE CHEERS AND CHANTS

Shouting personalized cheers and chants is a great way to show support for a team. If a team doesn't already have its own cheers and chants, cheerleaders can write some themselves. Writing cheers and chants can be a fun team activity. Teams can brainstorm ideas for cheers or watch other cheerleading teams to gain inspiration.

Some cheerleading teams add a player's name into a chant to show the player support.

PERSONALIZE IT!

When writing cheers and chants for a team, cheerleaders can include details that relate to their team or school. Using the name of a team's mascot or a team's colors in a cheer helps make it unique. Another way to personalize a cheer is to mention an opponent's team name, mascot, or colors.

Cheerleaders hold up signs to tell the audience what to cheer.

The details in the cheer or chant can change with every game to match each opponent.

Cheers and chants can also be written for different times during a game. Cheerleaders can shout different cheers depending on what their team is doing. For example, cheerleaders for a football team might use different cheers depending on which team has the ball.

PROPS AND ROUTINES

Using props is another way to personalize common cheers and chants. Popular cheerleading

POM-POMS

Cheerleading pom-poms are popular props. They were first created to help cheerleaders get a crowd's attention. The first poms were made in the 1930s by tying bright paper onto sticks. Today, most poms are made of plastic or foil.

Cheerleaders often perform after their team scores.

props include pom-poms, signs, flags, and megaphones. These can be designed to match a team's colors. When cheerleaders use props, they make an ordinary cheer or chant into something extraordinary.

Dancing and stunts can also make cheers and chants feel unique. A squad's routines can change with each game. That way, even people who go to every game will see something new with each performance.

There are many ways to make cheers and chants unique to each cheerleading squad. Using personalized cheers, props, and routines during games can help energize crowds and teams.

Cheerleaders use cheers and chants to rally crowds and raise team spirits. Whether they're performing a popular chant or a personalized cheer, cheerleaders know how to support their teams. With their exciting chants and cheers and unique routines, they're sure to energize any crowd.

GLOSSARY

choreography
The planned skills and movements in a routine.

coordinated
Moving and speaking together, often by using a shout, motion, or device.

customized
Made for a specific person or team.

halftime
The break after half of a game has been played.

mascot
A symbol such as an animal, object, or historical figure that represents a team.

megaphone
A cone-shaped prop used to make someone's voice louder.

personalize
To make something unique or give it a personal touch.

prop
An object such as a pom-pom, flag, or megaphone that is used to enhance a cheerleader's routine.

routine
A performance made up of individual stunts, tumbling moves, jumps, and dance moves.

squad
A cheerleading team.

stunt
A skill in which a cheerleader is supported above the ground by one or more teammates.

stutter
A speech disorder in which a person repeats sounds when talking.

synchronized
Performed at the same time as another person.

MORE INFORMATION

BOOKS

James, India. *Cheer Skills and Drills*. Abdo, 2025.

Mooney, Carla. *Competitive Cheerleading*. Abdo, 2025.

Troupe, Thomas Kingsley. *Cheerleading*. Crabtree, 2022.

ONLINE RESOURCES

To learn more about cheers and chants, please visit abdobooklinks.com or scan this QR code. These links are routinely monitored and updated to provide the most current information available.

INDEX

ABOUT THE AUTHOR

India James writes nonfiction for young readers. She loves learning and writing about new things. James lives in Ohio with her family.